African Magic Series

LUCUMI
THE WAYS OF SANTERIA

MONIQUE JOINER SIEDLAK

Oshun
Publications

Lucumi: The Ways of Santeria © 2018 Monique Joiner Siedlak

All rights reserved.

This book or parts thereof may not be reproduced in any form, stored in any retrieval system, or transmitted in any form by any means—electronic, mechanical, photocopy, recording, or otherwise—without prior written permission of the publisher, except as provided by United States of America copyright law.

Under no circumstances will any blame or legal responsibility be held against the publisher, or author, for any damages, reparation, or monetary loss due to the information contained within this book. Either directly or indirectly.

ISBN-13: 978-1-948834-84-1

Publisher:

Oshun Publications, LLC

Legal Notice:

This book is copyright protected. This book is only for personal use. You cannot amend, distribute, sell, use, quote or paraphrase any part, or the content within this book, without the consent of the author or publisher.

Disclaimer Notice:

Please note the information contained within this document is for educational and entertainment purposes only. All effort has been executed to present accurate, up to date, and reliable, complete information. No warranties of any kind are declared or implied. Readers acknowledge that the author is not engaging in the rendering of legal, financial, medical or professional advice. The content within this book has been derived from various sources. Please consult a licensed professional before attempting any techniques outlined in this book.

By reading this document, the reader agrees that under no circumstances is the author responsible for any losses, direct or indirect, which are incurred as a result of the use of information contained within this document, including, but not limited to, — errors, omissions, or inaccuracies.

Cover Design by MJS

Cover Image by Pixabay.com

Other Books in Series

African Spirituality Beliefs and Practices
Hoodoo
Seven African Powers: The Orishas
Cooking for the Orishas

Want to learn about African Magic, Wicca, or even Reiki while cleaning your home, exercising, or driving to work? I know it's tough these days to simply find the time to relax and curl up with a good book. This is why I'm delighted to share that I have books available in audiobook format.

Best of all, you can get the audiobook version of this book or any other book by me for free as part of a 30-day Audible trial.

Members get free audiobooks every month and exclusive discounts. It's an excellent way to explore and determine if audiobook learning works for you.

If you're not satisfied, you can cancel anytime within the trial period. You won't be charged, and you can still keep your book. To choose your free audiobook, visit:

www.mojosiedlak.com/free-audiobooks

WANT UPDATES, FREEBIES & GIVEAWAYS?!

MONIQUE JOINER SIEDLAK

THE ORISHAS

JOIN MY NEWSLETTER!

mojosiedlak.com/newsletter-signup

Contents

The Birth of Santeria	xi
1. Integration of Christianity	1
2. Is Voodoo and Santeria the Same?	5
3. The Concept of God in Santeria	9
4. Initiations	35
5. The Sacrifice of Santeria	41
6. Divination Practices in Santeria	45
7. Spells	49
8. Terms Used In Santeria	53
Conclusion	63
About the Author	65
Other Books by Monique Joiner Siedlak	67
Please Review	69

The Birth of Santeria

Santeria, The Way of Saints, is also known as La Regla de Ocha or The Order of the Orishas, is a religion whose origins can be traced back to the Yoruban tribes of West Africa. They were then later brought into the United States and Latin American countries through the transatlantic slave trade. It is practiced in Cuba and the Latin American countries, these days but has over 20,000 followers in the United States.

History of the Origin of Santeria

Santeria, as mentioned before, was brought into prominence when slaves from Yoruban tribes were brought into the Americas. The slaves brought over from West Africa clung to their culture and religions, even though their beliefs were criminalized by law. These slaves were then forced to convert to Christianity and worship the Christian God. These slaves clung to their religion and their individual spirituality as an escape to the harsh conditions they had to face in plantations.

In Cuba, the slaves clung to their religion and integrated aspects of Christianity and the saints into their practices. These old religions had a complex political and societal structure behind them, but this was all lost when the slaves were brought over to the Americas. The name Santeria originates from the worship of patron saints in Christianity, an act that was integrated into the old Yoruban religions.

ONE

Integration of Christianity
―――――――――――――

This integration was because slaves hid their actual religious practices from their slave masters. They used Christianity as a veil or front to worship their own saints. They used saints' days as a mask to worship and praise their own Orishas and their Spanish colonial masters thought they were taking an interest in Christianity.

This hiding or veiling became a historical and paved way for the religion to thrive among the slaves in Spanish colonial camps. The fact that many saints or santeros in Cuba, the Dominican Republic, and Puerto Rico were Roman Catholics helped the slaves to hide their religion and prove to the slave masters they were in fact interested with Christianity.

Santeria more or less remained within these parts but thrived. However, it slowly spread to the Caribbean and then later on to the United States when in 1959 the Cuban Revolution was taking place. Santeria spread rapidly in the United States so much so that the first Church of Santeria, the Church of the Lucumi Babalú Aye opened in 1974 in the United States.

. . .

Current Day Santeria

Santeria still continues in many of the Latin American countries. Cuba, Colombia, parts of Mexico, Venezuela, Panama and Puerto Rico all have a majority of people who practice the religion. As of 2001, there were upwards of 20,000 people who practiced the religion in the United States.

Santeria was brought into public view when issues with animal sacrifice were brought to court. The main Church of Santeria, the Church of the Lucumi Babalu Aye was taken to court as its animal sacrifices were deemed unconstitutional. Again in 2009 one of the members was taken to court in Texas but ended up winning as the member was found to be practicing their religion freely and any act to bar it would infringe on their freedom of religion.

Santeria is Not a Sinister Religion

Santeria is repeatedly portrayed as an evil cult that worships the Devil, demons and such. That the participants join in blood-thirsty rituals and attempts to harm others. This is deeply racist, colonial representation of the wonderful and complex African spiritual culture of Santeria. Santeria's main doctrine is to constantly seek to remain in a place of blessings or ire by adhering to the guidance of their egun, elders and the Orishas. There is a powerful morality of supporting others and working together to raise individuals out of hardship and disease toward strength, success, blessings, and endurance. They pray for the blessings of prosperity, blessings of children, and blessings of long life. They strive to develop a good character, live peaceful lives and respect nature and others around us. There is the use of magick for one's protection, but this does not differ from praying to God for defense against your foes or petitioning saints to block those who want to wrong you.

The issue is a need for knowledge with the scarcity of

information. As long as the society believe prejudiced stereotypes and don't educate them regarding the African Traditional Religions, they will persist in fearing Santeria. Working actively toward demystifying Santeria Lucumi through educational efforts, is the Santeria Church of the Orishas. They help individuals know and understand what they actually believe and what they actually do.

TWO

Is Voodoo and Santeria the Same?

All too frequently, Santeria is mistakenly confused amidst different African stemmed magickal or religious practices. It is very simple for individuals to relate to the systems of Santeria Lucumi as "voodoo" by the movies and the news. This cross-confusion between Voodoo and Hoodoo and you see an entirely different layer of misinterpretation concerning what Santeria actually is.

Both Santeria and Voodoo are both religions, however they are not alike. Voodoo is more accurately two chief parts to Vodou, Haitian Vodou, and New Orleans or Louisiana Vodoun.

Haitian Vodou is an African dispersed religion that originated collectively of the traditional African religious customs of numerous tribes. Many of who were adversaries made to survive and depend on one another because of the conditions of slavery. The Yoruba tribe was amongst them that endured in Haiti. These individuals merged their customs in an attempt to withstand and designed a ritual in order to worship and provide each tribe's spirits during their time of honor. These customs were likewise determined through syncretism by Catholic French. Confirmation of this can be perceived by the association of Catholic saint pictures to symbolize the spirits or Loa honored in Vodou. The Loa of Vodou is made of the Rada Loa, the Petro Loa, and the Guede Loa. Veves or adorned cornmeal designs placed out on the ground or on tables are utilized to request the Loa in Vodou, however not in Santeria. Haitian Vodou does have an initiated clergy, except initiation is not a condition for participation in the belief and the huge majority of Vodouisants are not initiates. A magickal charm package, also known as wanga and gris-gris bag is often used in Haitian Vodou's magic. Haitian Creole, Haitian Vodou's principal traditional language is the local dialect of Haitian French.

Remember, Santeria emerged in Cuba. It is embedded in the African religious customs of the Yoruba people. The disciples of Santeria worship the Orishas, the demi-gods of the Yoruba communities. For the outsider, there is a semblance of Spanish Catholicism that aspect quickly slips away once an individual has experienced initiation. A separate religious practice, Espiritismo, brings the primary engagement of Catholic elements that has remained profoundly entwined into Santeria. Santeria is highly initiatory, secretive and operates under strict spiritual practices. Presence in the religion is extremely limited to those who are not initiated and the vast majority of members are initiated. Santeria does not use or fancy made images to request to the Orishas as done in Voodoo. Lucumi is the primary language of Santeria. Infused with the aspects of Cuban Spanish, Lucumi is a dialect of the Yoruban language.

The religious procedures and magickal workings of these spiritual rituals may have parallels but they are absolutely not the same thing. An individual which is initiated in Santeria will not possess the religious favors or permission to take part in Vodou rituals, but a Vodou initiate would. On the other hand, an individual initiated in Vodou would not have the permission and rights to take a role in a Santeria ceremony.

Each of these religions varies from one another, and each uses specific languages, songs, rituals, pleas, and invocations from the others. The only commonality linking them is the custom of animal sacrifice and the usage of magickal spell work as an integral part of their religious practice. In sub-Saharan Africa, this is common with any religious practice.

THREE

The Concept of God in Santeria

Olodumare is neither masculine nor feminine, but sexually neutral. As an all-knowing, all-powerful divinity, it was Olodumare who created the earth and the entire universe. It is said the Orishas are Olodumare's eldest children, ingrained with a quantity of her Ashe. The Orishas are demigods who have been sent to look after humanity. They oversee the forces of nature besides our burdens. Because Olodumare has moved on to form new universes, we worship and honor her but direct our worship around the Orishas and our relationship with them.

Before the slave trade, each large city in the Yoruba country was a center of devotion for a particular Orisha. During the period where the slaves were intermixed and forced to coexist outside their countries of origin, the custom of these Orishas became blended, and their prayer of multiple Orishas became the standard form within La Regla Lucumi or Santeria. As a transformation of our initiation service, within Lucumi practice, they ordain new initiates into the faiths of multiple Orishas instead of just one as was performed in Africa. Every person ordained as a priest or priestess receives the secrecies of Chango, Obatala, Oshun,

Ellegua, and Yemaya, when they are inducted. If their tutelary Orisha differs from those five, they will accept that Orisha as well. While they get the mysteries of multiple Orishas, they inaugurate them with their tutelary Orisha and serve as a living agent of that Orisha's spirit walking amongst us all.

The Orishas recognize each other and are described by their individual colors, numbers, markings, feasts, and temperaments. These items direct what gifts and offerings are acceptable for each specific Orisha. The supporters of all the Orishas will make donations in the manner in which they are used to so that the Orishas acknowledge and will give an answer in the appearance of a spell or curse. Understanding the forces of nature that guide them, the Orishas can be best understood. For example, we can find Elegua at the crossroads, while Oshun enjoys the rivers.

Babalu Aye: The God of Diseases

Extremely feared and well-respected, Babalu Aye is the Lord of many diseases. Babalu Aye is also known as Omulu, Azojano, San Lazaro and Shanpana. Often times, he is associated with the sun because the sun is a source of life in some places but also a source of death in some. He is also specifically known as the Lord of Smallpox. Medicines and vaccines have reduced the contraction of smallpox. However, Babalu Aye continues to strike people with diseases such as AIDS/HIV, tuberculosis, Ebola, etc.

Babalu Aye is a muscular man who covers himself with straw and walks with the help of a staff. The straw he uses to cover himself up is to hide his smallpox. He can make any person sick as a punishment, which is why he is so feared. However, he can also help cure that person, which is why people respect him. No one in the African Diaspora wants to get on the bad side of Babalu Aye and be afflicted with life-threatening diseases.

Many stories and sources will make you perceive Babalu Aye as a feared Orisha. However, Babalu Aye is also a very merciful Orisha. He can cure you as quickly as he can make you contract a disease. Sometimes when people suffer from life-threatening diseases, they wish for death for peace. Babalu Aye helps grant them their wish and helps to guide those souls over to the other side. Babalu Aye is often found in hospitals, hospices, places where people are cured, gyms and the desert as well.

Some traditions tell that Babalu Aye contracted smallpox as a punishment from the God Olofi. He was punished for being disobedient and not having a nice character. He lost all his wealth and riches. His trials on this earth are a lesson of humility, perseverance, patience and good character. Babalu Aye is loving but extremely strict as well.

Babalu Aye is also the protector of all animals, especially dogs. Apart from Elegua, who was his only companion while he suffered through his trials, dogs also accompanied him and provided companionship.

Babalu Aye's lineage is not exactly known. While most people believe that he is the son of Yemaya, his relationship with Nana Buruku is where many people get confused. Some say that she is his wife and some say that she is his mother. A majority of people believe that Nana Buruku is Babalu Aye's mother. Babalu Aye is very commonly associated with Osain who is the herb Orisha. This is because of Babalu Aye's knowledge of how plants can heal people.

The ceremony for worshipping Babalu Aye is known as the Awan in the Santeria tradition. Burlap is sacred to this Orisha and is often offered as a sacrifice to him. Babalu Aye's sacred number is 17 and his sacred colors are purple, brown and yellow. December 17th is Babalu Aye's day. His favorite food offerings are a roasted ear of corn, popcorn, black-eyed peas, rum, tobacco, and beans.

. . .

Obatala: Father Figure of the Orishas

Obatala is known to be a wise Orisha and is often also known as the chief and judge. He is married to Yemeya, who is the mother figure of all Orishas and is the Goddess of the Oceans. According to some patakis, Obatala is the father of all human beings. He and Yemeya created a lot of children. One day he got very drunk when making humans because he was thirsty and he drank some palm wine. Under the influence of the wine, he made some deformed humans. Once he able to think clearly, he recognized what he had done. He swore from that day that he would never drink and now every handicapped or deformed person has a special place in his heart. He takes extra care of them. Obatala shows mercy and compassion because of the fact that he realizes that he erred once when he got drunk on the palm wine. This is why he is also known to be the fairest Orisha of all.

Obatala was a very strong warrior when he was young and saw many injustices and wrongs being committed during those wars. Which is why when he became an Orisha, he vouched for peace. His experience on the battlefields angered him and now, as a judge, he is very much involved in the law and issues of justice. He will be involved in any kind of legal case or court issue. You can invoke him during such times for his help. However, do not invoke him if you are guilty unless you are willing to be punished for it. Obatala is also involved in karmic justice. If you think someone has done a karmic injustice to you, you can call to him for help. He will help you and make you be strong. He encourages humans to take responsibility for their irrational actions.

Obatala has no gender and is thought to be asexual. This is why he is rightfully thought to be the father of human beings. He has no patience for the gender fights which break out in the human community.

Obatala is also associated with the color white. He is known as the God of white clothing and even loves his food to be white in color. He loves white offerings with no spices or even alcohol. People tend to spread a white cotton ball on the offerings they make to Obatala to please him. People can even offer him eggs, rice, mushrooms, water, milk, crushed egg shells, snail shells, myrrh or tobacco. Obatala worshippers dance in white costumes and offer white pumpkin, coconut milk and light up sandalwood incense to please this Orisha.

Obatala is often found in churches, libraries, universities, mountains, forest and the military. His number is 8 and his feast day is the 24th of September. His tool is a horsetail fly whisk. All of the animals sacrificed to Obatala should be white in color such as she-goats, guinea hens, doves, and hens.

Ogun: The Orisha of Iron

Ogun is known as Oggun, Ogou or Ogum. He is said to be a very powerful warrior who has creativity and intelligence when it comes to making new tools. He protects his people from injustice. He is known as the father of civilization because if it were not for his creative tools, the earth would be full of the wilderness. If it were not for his strength, the path from heaven to earth would never have been cleared for the Orishas and humanity to thrive on earth. Ogun's tools were the tools which helped create new buildings and cities.

Ogun has a protective nature, like a loving and overprotective father. He can be the fiercest and angriest bloodthirsty warrior whose tools thirst for the blood of his enemies. However, he can also be the Orisha who helps removes cancers from humans and forges new innovative tools. Ogun is very loyal and is often found in densely forested areas where he likes to hunt with his best-hunting partners, Ellegua and Ochosi. These three signifies one of the Orishas to be received during the reception of the Warriors initiation. Ogun's shrine is an iron cauldron which is filled with iron tools and supplements.

Ogun is the one who invented the knife, though, he does not own it. It is Obatala who owns it. Ogun was just asked to make the knife for him. It is with Ogun's strong and piercing energy that animals are sacrificed. This way, it is not the olorisha who takes the animal's life, it is Ogun. This is often reflected in the phrase which people recite before sacrificing an animal: "Ogun shoro shoro, eyebale kuwo".

There is a Pataki related to Ogun which tells how he became the Orisha of iron. The Orishas and humans were once living on the land created by Obatala. Orishas and the humans alike leveled the land and cleared the trees from the land so that they could cultivate on it. However, the problem arose when, as the population began to increase, they needed more land for the people to live and build houses on. Their tools, however, were not enough. They were made of wood, stone or soft metal. So, all the Orishas met and decided to clear the land with their tools one by one. All except Olokun disagreed, saying that she had nothing to do with the land and that her domain was the oceans and seas. Osanyin, Orisha of medicine, decided to clear the field first. However, his bush knife was made of soft metal and it became bent. The same happened with Oko and Eshu. Seeing the Orishas fail, Ogun with his iron knife set out and cleared the land and fields. He came back showing his undamaged knife. He declined to give the secret of iron to the other Orishas. The Orishas offered to make him their ruler for which he agreed and gave them the knowledge of iron. However one day he was cast out because he looked messy, muddy and bloody. The Orishas rejected him but the people, to this day, still remember and worship him.

The use of technology and science in warfare is the sphere of Ogun along with blacksmithing, farming, civilization in general, and transportation. Once Elegua opens the doors and roads, Ogun then cleanses them with his machete. His number is seven and his color scheme is red and white in Voodoo, while green and black in Santeria.

Ogun's Yoruban feast day is January 17th, while April 23rd is the day in Santeria. His food offerings are typically meat, nuts, chili, peppers, hot and spicy foods, roots and soda crackers with palm oil, rum, and whiskey.

Chango: King of the Religion
Also spelled and pronounced as Shango, Chango is a very important Orisha in Santeria. He is one of the four pillars in Santeria and every person has to receive him during initiation, whether they are his children or not. Apart from being the King of the religion on earth, Chango is also the Orisha for male virility, leadership, thunder, fire, drumming, and dancing. Chango was known to not be as effective as a king should be when he was alive. However, after his death, he worked miracles for the other Orishas. Chango is also known to have had many female lovers and was an exquisite dancer and drummer. Chango also has a magical and powerful mortar which allows him to spit fire from his mouth. A double-headed ax is his favorite weapon and his residence is at the top of the royal palm tree.

There is a popular Pataki related to Chango and Oya. Chango was once at a party, drinking and dancing and enjoying the time of his life. Chango had enjoyed so much that he did not realize that some of his adversaries were outside of the party watching him. As soon as the party died down and all the guests left, Chango staggered to a corner where an enemy was waiting for him. The enemy quickly trapped him and locked him in a small cell. At that time, Chango and Oya had had a fling. He had kept his pilon and mortar at her house. Days passed and Oya grew worried because Chango did not show up. Oya began to wonder about his pilon and mortar. She saw that the inside of the mortar was gleaming and a clear liquid formed. She saw the Chango was trapped in a cell and became furious. She quickly called upon lightning to help her rescue Chango. She kissed the liquid in the mortar and soon her lips and mouth started burning. No water could ease the burning and fire started spitting out. The lightning came and took her to Chango. As she reached there, Oya screamed a war shout and an explosion of fire spewed from her mouth.

Chango's enemies soon dispersed and Oya released Chango. She told him about how she rescued him as he could not remember. Chango was upset that Oya interfered, but was grateful. Ever since then, Oya now accompanies Chango in fights and wars.

Chango fathered the Ibeji twins as well Boromu and Borosia, the children born because of Yegua rape. Many Orishas used to complain about Chango's unruly and egoistic attitude. However, through many trials and errors and a reality check from Obatala, Chango soon matured and learned gracefulness and charm. This Orisha teaches us that no matter how many mistakes we make, we can always turn around and redeem ourselves. He is very loving and compassionate towards his children and all Orishas.

His colors are red, white and gold. His numbers are 4 or 6 or both. Honor Chango with martial arts, fire, and dance on December 3rd Spicy foods, alcohol, chili peppers, tobacco, okra, and cornbread make great offerings for this Orisha.

Oshun: The Orisha of Love

Oshun is appropriately recognized as the Orisha of love because she was the last Orisha to be born out of the love Olodumare had for creations. Many people compare Oshun to the Greek God Aphrodite. This is because Oshun is not simply the Orisha of Love but also femininity, beauty, and sexuality. Oshun is known to usually live near rivers.

Oshun is very popularly celebrated in Africa, especially by women. This is because she represents each and every aspect of a woman's life. Often times, she is portrayed as a woman of mixed race with long locks of hair carrying a fan and a mirror. This illustrates her beauty. Oshun is further acknowledged to be a powerful sorceress. Some claim that she seduces her lovers by weaving different spells to trap them in. Oshun loves Aña drums. Whenever she feels sorrowful, she dances to forget her worries. Oshun is a very loving and protective Orisha but she is also known to turn cruel and furious against those who disrespect her or her children. Forgiveness by this Orisha is very hard to expect. It is also said that whenever Oshun possesses her olorishas if they appear crying then it is a good sign. Crying means that the tears are tears of joy. If the olorishas appear laughing, it is a bad sign. The laughing is maniacal laughing, which represents her anger.

Oshun is also popularly known as the mother of the Ibeji, the twin Orishas, which were fathered by Chango. She was accused of being a witch for mothering the twins after which she kicked out the Ibeji twins. The twins were then adopted by Oya (some say that they were adopted by Yemeya). Oshun was then destitute and cursed. However, she was soon blessed with another child by Olofi which was named Ideu.

There is also a Pataki related to Oshun and Iroko. Oshun was once preparing for a party. She dressed herself up in gold, jewelry, and perfumes and passed by a small village where some small children were playing. She was happy when she saw them and sprinkled honey on them, after which they bowed to her. Oshun sat down near Iroko, a Cieba Tree when a tear dropped. Iroko asked Oshun what was wrong, to which she replied that she missed having children and wanted Iroko to help her bear children. Iroko agreed to the price that Oshun must accompany Iroko every now and then to which she agreed.

Oshun bore a son and Iroko, hearing about the good news, asked Oshun. Oshun only replied that yes, she had given birth to a son and kept walking, forgetting her promise.

Every now and then she would promise Iroko that she would bring a goat or bring her son to meet him. One day, Ideu sat under Iroko and told him that he was the son of Oshun. Becoming happy, he brought Ideu to his domain to tell him stories. Years passed and Oshun could not find her son. Iroko saw how depressed Oshun was and soon brought Ideu back to Oshun. After which, Oshun's children were never allowed to meet Iroko.

The Feast of Oshun is September 8: However, in Nigeria, it falls on the last Friday of August in the town of Oshogbo, whose official Orisha is Oshun.

Oya: Queen of the Cemetery

A female warrior, Oya is an extremely powerful warrior. She is the owner of the marketplace and guards the door of the cemetery. Being a warrior, she rides into battle while wielding lightning and her machetes. She is often accompanied to battle by her favorite lover, Chango. Oya can raise the army of the dead during a fight or a battle and patakis often say that Oya has used tornados as a weapon. Many patakis say Oya is literally a tornado.

Oya is like a compassionate but stern mother. She is recognized to give her children and worshippers some space to cry and gripe about their troubles and get it all off of their chests. However, she expects you to pull it together. She will steer you along the path and help you with the difficulties and challenges you encounter. However, she will not do the actual work for you as she requires you yourself to do it. Oya is also perceived to be a witch. She is comfortable around occult objects and is claimed to have strong links with the ancestors. Which is why she should be involved in any and every ancestral ceremony.

Oya guards the cemeteries. It is her fundamental role to keep away the grave robbers and disrespecters of the ancestors. She will hunt them down mercilessly and punish them for it.

Oya is known to be the third wife of Chango. Chango chose Oya to be his wife after his first wife, Oba, and second wife, Oshun, had a feud and big rivalry between them which blew up into a war. Chango, after that incident, wanted a much more balanced and supportive woman. According to some patakis, Oya and Chango never lived together. Oya loved her peace and liked living in the forests. Already tired of rivalries between women, Chango was a busy man. Both of them gave each other space however they loved each other fiercely. Till they died, they always stayed connected.

People often tend to find lessons in these patakis and stories of Oya and Chango. The most common lesson is that when people are young, they find familial duty and sexual attraction to be the most important aspects. Which is why Chango first wife was a dutiful woman and his second wife was very visually stunning. However, with time and age, once we have settled and become well established, all we look for is pleasure and peace. Our priorities change, just like Chango's when he chose Oya to be his wife. So, a woman who wants to be her husband's everything should learn to balance Chango's three wives: Obba, Oshun, and Oya.

There are different views on the way Oya looks. Some say she is so incredibly beautiful that she has to wear a veil to hide her beauty from men. Some say she wears a veil because she has a scarred, burnt and horrendous face which, if anyone looked at, would die.

Feast of Oya is February 2nd. Oya enjoys dark colored and sweet foods as her offering.

Ellegua: Lord of the Crossroads

Ellegua is known by numerous names such as Elegba, Legba, Papa Legba, Eshu, Esu or Elewa. He is one of the most important Orishas to exist. He is acknowledged to be the first Orisha to be created by Olodumare herself. He is recognized to be the Lord of the Crossroads because, without him, our prayers to the other Orishas would never pass. He illustrates the start and end of existence and the opening and closing passages of life. Which is why when people worship or make offerings to the other Orishas; they make certain to make an offering to Ellegua as well to have his blessing. He facilitates divination by connecting to the other Orishas for us. Otherwise, the gates of communication with the other Orishas would remain closed.

Ellegua is also very frequently seen as the trickster, troublemaker or even experimenter. This is because he loves to test humanity. He is a witness to all a man speaks or does and he tests our word, the integrity, and sincerity. This is why people know him as a trickster. During the reception of the Warriors in an initiation, Ellegua is the first Orisha to be received before Oshun, Ochosi, and Ogun. He can speak for all of the other Orishas which is why people tend to make him an offering first before the others. He is recognized as the most crucial and important Orisha during such rites.

Ellegua is regularly represented as a child and sometimes an old man. He is represented as a child because he is known to like child-like things such as toy soldiers, balls, whistles and even candies. Apart from the childish things, he likes silver coins and is often depicted as wearing a straw hat or a red kerchief. Ellegua's colors are mainly red and black. His lucky number is 3 and any multiple of 3. His day of the week is Monday and the 3rd day of each month. In Cuba, Ellegua has saint days on the 6th of January and 13th of June. On these days, the people of Cuba throw a huge feast to honor this Orisha.

Apart from candy, this Orisha is also known to like toasted corn, strong alcohol, rum, vino seco, cigars, smoked hutia meat, smoked fish and red palm oil. These foods make a great offering for him and people often tend to offer these foods to the Orisha on Mondays. Ellegua is also the most sexual entity. His statue is often represented him as having an erect penis.

Ellegua, Eshu, and The Pomba Gira are thought to be separate entities but are closely related. Many people like to think of the three of them as siblings. Ellegua is thought to be the most important out of all three which why he is made an offering first. The rest of the two follow after Ellegua. All the world's doorways, whether physical or emotional, are controlled by them. They can make a person the luckiest in the world or they can make a person the unluckiest person on earth. It all depends on them.

Ochosi: The Hunter

Ochosi, also known and spelled as Oxosi, Oshosi, is a great and stealthy hunter who lives in the woods. He is not only known for his great hunting skills, he is also a fisherman, a warrior with great arrow skills, a seer with shamanistic powers and a magician. Ochosi is also the lord of justice and the defender/patron of those who has had misdoings with the law.

Ochosi, during his time, was only a huntsman who became an Orisha. According to a sacred story, also known as a Pataki, Ochosi was once given a task by Elegua. He was asked to hunt a rare bird for Orula who wanted to gift the bird to Olofi. Since Ochosi was a skilled hunter and had no problems finding his prey, he agreed and caught the rare bird in a matter of minutes. He caged it and brought it back home. Immediately he informed Orula that he had caught the bird. As Ochosi went out, his mother came home to find the bird in a cage and thought that Ochosi had caught it for dinner. She killed the bird and dressed it. She then went out to the local market to buy some condiments to cook it with. During this time, Ochosi came home to find that the bird had been killed to his great sorrow and anger. However, he had no time to worry about who killed it since he had already informed Orula of the bird. He went out to catch another one of those rare birds and was successful. Ochosi then accompanied Orula and gave the bird to Olofi. Olofi was so delighted with the gift that he gave Ochosi a crown and made him an Orisha right there. Olofi then asked Ochosi whether there was anything else he wished for. Ochosi demanded to shoot an arrow into the air and have it pierced the heart of whoever killed the first bird. Since Olofi was the all-knowing, he asked Ochosi whether he was sure that that was what he wanted. Ochosi replied in the affirmative, saying that he wanted justice. Olofi granted his wish and as soon as Ochosi shot an arrow into the air, he heard his mother scream and cry out in pain. Once Ochosi realized what he had done, he was disheartened, but he knew that justice had been served. This is why Olofi made it Ochosi's task to hunt for the truth and serve justice where ever he went.

According to certain Patakis, Ochosi is known to live in an iron cauldron with Ogun. Eleguà, Ogun, and Ochosi are said to be brothers, although all of them had different mothers. According to Pataki, Ogun and Ochosi weren't always on good terms. However, they set aside their differences for the greater good. Forests were dense, which made hunting hard. Ochosi and Ogun made a pact where Ochosi would hunt and Ogun would clear the path for him. This is why now they are known to be inseparable.

Ochosi's day is June 6th and his numbers are 3, 4, and 7. His tools are 3 arrows, 3 hunting dogs, and a fish hook.

Oko: The Farmer

Oko, also known as Orishaoco or Orishaoko, is perceived to be the Orisha for farming, agriculture, fertility and the secret of life and death. Orisha Oko is acknowledged to be the

Orisha with the hardest job and tiring work. This is because he has to farm and feed the people and Orishas on the Earth year round. The Orisha Oko is beseeched by humans to generally keep death away, for good health, a stable life and for conceiving a child.

Orisha Oko is recognized to be the ex-husband of Yemaya. Yemaya, also known as Agganba, is the daughter of the Orisha of the sea. According to a Pataki, one day Orisha Oko was walking near the sea when his eyes caught sight of a lovely woman. The woman was Agganba, daughter of the Orisha of the sea, Olokun. Oko wanted to marry her immediately but Agganba told him that she was unable to leave the sea because she had defects and people would make fun of her. Orisha Oko promised to never make fun of her and love her as she was. Oko and Agganba then got married. According to some stories, Agganba was considered to be a mermaid with no legs or was thought to be completely deformed. For many years, Oko and Agganba lived contentedly until one day Agganba found out that Oko had been talking about her deformities to other people. Filled with such rage, she left Oko and told him that the ocean and harvest would never have any contact. She cursed that his animals would turn against him and his harvest will die. Olokun, enraged by what Oko had done, almost sent a wave to destroy Oko's lands and harvests. Oko immediately made many sacrifices for Olokun to escape his wrath. Olokun agreed to destroy his lands but Agganba never came back to Oko and his harvests grow far from the ocean.

Orisha Oko's name means 'Orisha of the farm', sometimes even known as 'Orisha of the penis'. This is because his temple/shrine is covered with phallic symbols of two coconuts and a dowel, representing the male genitalia. Orisha Oko's sacred objects are painted red and white, to depict fertility from blood and semen.

Orisha Oko is known to adore root vegetables. They make

the perfect offering for him. Sweet potatoes, yams, corn, taro roots, etc. are great offerings for him. Animals such as guinea hens, pigeons, and roosters are said to be the perfect sacrificial animals for Orisha Oko as an offering. Many people tend to offer ñame (nya-meh) as an offering to Orisha Oko to please him. Ñame are white yams which should be boiled, mashed, made into balls, dabbed with palm oil, drizzled with honey and sprinkled with smoked fish or toasted corn. Roasted sweet potatoes are also known to be a great offering for Orisha Oko. Roast them and dab them with palm oil.

Orisha Oko's feast day is either March 22nd or May 15th, while his number is 7. His sacred places are plowed fields and black fertile earth. His sacred tool is a plow pulled by a group of oxen.

Olokun- The Goddess of the Deep Seas

Olokun is more commonly known as a feminine deity. However, many also choose to interpret her as a male deity. Her name literally means owner (olo) of the waters (okun). Olokun is, nowadays, associated with the deep seas, the literal bottom floors of the seas. While Yemaya is the Goddess who is linked to the top of the ocean, where sunlight reaches and photosynthesis takes place.

Olokun's realm is known as the Land of the Dead. Dead Sea creatures eventually drop down to the surface of the sea, providing sustenance to other sea creatures. This process of dying and dropping is also known as 'marine snow'. Due to the great pressure at the bottom and the darkness, many sea creatures thriving there tend to have monstrous forms. Olokun's Queendom has almost never been seen by the human eye properly, as no one can dive down that deep into the sea. Olokun is often also known as the Goddess of secrets because whatever dies in the sea is never or rarely ever found. This is why she also signifies wisdom. The fact that there is always something worth knowing even if you cannot attain its knowledge, especially about birth, life, death and the Afterlife. Olokun also presides over meditation, mental health, dreaming, psychic abilities and water-based healing. Many women pray to her for conceiving a child.

Olokun is also associated with great wealth. People that want power worship Olokun for exactly that purpose.

Although most females tend to worship Olokun, the legend stories tell that men were the initial worshippers of Olokun.

The first legends tell us about a hunter who resided in Urhoniigbe. To determine the origin of distant singing, he ventured off into the woods and found a King including his court. He was invited by the King to participate in a spiritual ceremony for which the hunter agreed. He decided to stay with the King, Olokun, for almost three years and learned spiritual practices and worship associated with Olokun. Till that time, his friends and family presumed him to be dead. However, he returned to his people, carrying a water pot over his head. He was completely mute and couldn't speak. To the shock of the town's people, he started dancing. He was mocked for it but it only set down the 14-day event of ritualistic dancing to please Olokun. When the 14 days were over, he regained his ability to speak and told the townsfolk about his experiences. All criticism was erased when the hunter did spiritual work to please Olokun and his town was blessed with positivity. He was designated Chief Priest of Olokun and a temple for Olokun was built on the spot where the hunter had rested his water pot after the 14th day.

Olokun is often depicted as a black mermaid. The animal used to symbolize Olokun is the mudfish which buries itself in the mud. She is also linked to the red coral. The coral purifies the water and provides sustenance for sea animals.

· · ·

Ibeji: The Sacred Twins

Ibeji is also known as Ibelli, Ibryi, Meji, Melli, and Jimaguas. They are twins, but the Ibeji are identified as one Orisha. 'Ibi' accurately means born and 'eji' means two. Twins are considered to be very sacred among the people of Yoruba. They have the highest rate of twin births, about 5% whereas the rest of the world has a twin-birth percentage of 0.5%. The Ibeji and all twins of this world are considered to have one soul in two bodies. The Ibeji are believed to be the original twins born on this earth and are said to be the Orishas of joy, glee, and mischief. The Gemini twins in astrology are also said to be related directly to the Ibeji. The Ibejis parents are, namely, Chango and Oshun.

A traditional Pataki tells us the story of how Oshun was shunned when she gave birth to twins. This is because at that time giving birth to twins was deemed unusual. Only animals could give birth to multiple and the same looking babies. She was labeled as a witch and ousted from the community. Oshun, because she was afraid of being shunned, pushed the Ibeji out of her home and rejected being their mother. Thus began Oshun's depressive spiral, leading to a loss of wealth, stability and sanity. The Ibeji were adopted by Oya who was an Orisha as well. Oya loved children, but was unfortunately barren and could not bear children. She had had only one pregnancy which was stillborn. Anyone who receives and worships the Ibeji is known to be blessed with joy, happiness, and abundance. A Cuban Pataki even says that the Ibeji drove the devil and misfortune away by driving them insane with their bewitched drums.

The Ibeji are named Kehinde and Taiwo. The firstborn is named Taiwo and the second born is named Kehinde. Kehinde literally means 'the one who comes after'. Taiwo literally means 'the first to touch the surface' or 'the one who gets the first taste of the world'. Legends say that Kehinde is the firstborn. This is because Kehinde sends Taiwo out first to be born to check whether the conditions and situations of the Earth are normal. The Kehinde is said to have authority over the first-born twin which is why Kehinde is considered to be the first child. When the first child (Taiwo) is born, it cries. The crying delivers a spiritual message to the other twin. The cry carries the message of whether the situation is normal or not. If not, Kehinde may decide not to come out. Both of the twins may either decide not to continue and live their life or there may be one stillbirth. Kehinde is also known as 'omg gbegbon'. This literally means 'the elder who came out last.'

The number 11 is considered to be the number of the Ibeji. This is because the twins are complimenting as well as opposing forces. One Ibeji holds the human personality and the other holds the spiritual personality.

The feast day for Ibeji is usually celebrated on September 27th which is also the Catholic feast day of Cosmos and Damian. For offerings, give them sugarcane, fruit, and fruit juices. Don't forget the toys. They are, after all children.

Obba

First wife of Chango, the third king of the Oyo Empire, Obba represents the dutiful and devoted wife. Related to lagoons and lakes, she is known also as the Orisha of marriage and the home. It is to be noted that few Orishas were dutiful and devoted to their husband; thus, Obba holds her own importance among the other Orishas.

Apart from the dutiful and devoted wife, as stated above, Obba also represents the suffering and sacrifice one makes for their loved ones. This is why a famous sacrifice tale is associated with her in which she lost one of her ears.

It is known as that Chango was never satisfied with one woman. Obba knew of his passionate love affairs and was willing of accepting them in this condition that the other women in Chango's life were subordinates to her. However, the cases of Oshun and Oya were different. They were treated like queens by Chango. The love and passion Obba wanted for herself from Chango were being given on other Oshun and Oya. This situation made Obba frustrated. She was willing to do anything to win the love of Chango back.

One rival of Obba took advantage of her vulnerable state and played a trick on her. She convinced her that there was a certain way to win Chango's love back again. She made her believe that there is a magical component that should be used as an ingredient when she is cooking food for Chango. Upon eating that food, the love for Obba will boom in the heart of Chango magically.

This Orisha persuaded Obba to cut one of her ears, use it as a magical ingredient, and feed it to Chango as she made her believe that she does the same. She also convinced her that ears magically regenerate so that should have no fear of losing her ear.

Obba was hesitant at first, but decided to give it a try in order to become the most important Orisha in Chango's life. Ultimately, she cut her ear and presented her to Chango. Chango, when he arrived to pay a visit to Obba, he took notice of the bandage around the head of Obba. However, he didn't ask many questions as to what led to her injury.

Obba presented the cooker ear as an appetizer to Chango. Not only the sight of a cooker ear made him extremely angry but disgusted as well. He left Obba at that very moment and never returned back. Despite this story floating, it shouldn't be concluded that Obba was a submissive or passive wife. She was an intelligent woman who had a vast knowledge of politics and commerce.

In some parts of Africa, Obba is recognized as a guardian of prostitutes while in Brazil, they know her as a goddess of love. It is often believed that she favors those women who are dutiful to their husband and punishes those who are not loyal to their loved ones.

You can offer water which was taken from a lake or pond, wine, flowers or even beans with onions and shrimp on her feast day November 25th.

Yegua: Cemetery Queen

Known as the queen of Cadavers, Yegua, also known as Yewa, was a marina Orisha initially. She is now believed to guard corpses throughout the time of their funeral rites and when they are buried. After their burial, she then hands them over to Oya, her sister who is known as the Cemetery Queen. Most of the time, corpses are passed on to Oya when they have turned into the skeleton. During this whole duration, Yegua guards them. However, in some cases, she may also consume the corpses if allowed time by Oya.

Yegua is known to be the most beautiful daughter of Olokun. She, along with Olosa, ruled lagoons.

A common story floating related to Yegua is about her affair with Chango. It is known that Chango had a flamboyant personality and he was never satisfied with one woman. Thus, he would often cheat his legitimate, dutiful, and loyal wife Orisha Obba with other Orishas. During the younger days of Yegua, when she was a virgin, Chango had an eye on her. He seduced her secretly and, as a result, Yegua got pregnant with his child.

Boromu, another Orisha then convinced Yegua to consume an herbal potion. Yegua listened to his advice, but ended up aborting her child. The whole experience proved to be devastating for her. She chose a tree and buried the fetus beneath it. Due to this experience, she confined herself to the cemetery and became the Queen of Cadavers.

The whole event was then reported to Olokun by Boromu. Moreover, he also brought him to the tree Yegua chose to bury the fetus beneath. It is now believed that the unborn child, Borosia, came back to life in a spirit form. Many people also believe that he serves as a guard of the court owned by Olokun.

Orisha Yegua represents loneliness. Other characteristics associated with her include sterility, female chastity, and virginity. It is said that Yegua colors are pink, red, scarlet, and burgundy. Yegua wears a pink dress and a belt on it. As per studies, the nature of Yegua is very sweet yet she is strict with her children as she wants them to be perfect. She doesn't like the use of foul language and vulgarity.

When it comes to offerings to Yegua, it is believed that she should be offered flowers with a fragrance that to plenty of them so that the unpleasant odor coming out from the corpses she lives with can be reduced. Apart from fragrant flowers, Yegua can be offered young and virgin animals, tuna fish, and peanut balls. It is to be noted that only female animals must be offered to her.

Due to all these features and characteristics, Yegua is often regarded as a shadowy and reclusive Orisha.

Aggayu: Orisha of Volcanoes

While some individuals believe Aggayú is the Orisha of deserts while others believe him to be the Orisha of volcanoes. It is further believed he lived in a palm tree when he is facing a troublesome condition. Another confusion that floats around Aggayú relates to his relationship with Chango. As per some people, he is the younger brother of Chango. However, there is a certain section of people who believe him to be the father of Chango. Either way, both are regarded as inseparable and they share certain qualities and personalities.

Those who believe Aggayú to be the father of Chango, they are of the view he is protective by nature. Aggayú offers great support to others during their tough times. He has always taught others to be strong and level-headed.

It is believed Aggayú can create new lands using his forces.

Furthermore, he can also build new mountains and pathways for new rivers. Aggayú could ferry people across the rivers due to his abilities. It is believed Aggayú's raises his legs quite high when walking. This is why he takes long strides.

Various historians have written about the relationship Aggayú had with Oshun. Although Aggayú was known to have relationships with many Orishas; however, the love he had for Oshun is the most talked about. It so happen that he was helping people to move to the other part of the river, suddenly he fell in the water. Since he didn't know swimming, he started to drown in the river water. Oshun saved his life, and she used an oar and pulled him out of the water. This was the time he fell in love with her.

The ritual of "Chango Oro Aggayú" is performed to crown Aggayú to a person instead of being crowned in a kariocha ceremony. In this ritual process, Aggayú is placed on the shoulder of the person while Chango is placed on their head.

A major reason people believe this practice is followed that Aggayú cannot be crowned on a person's head since it wasn't placed on the head of the godparent. However, another reason cited for following this practice is that the energy of Aggayú is quite explosive or volatile. Hence, it cannot be directly placed on a person's head.

When making offerings for Aggayu, it is important to note that he likes to enjoy rich food since he has a strong appetite. Food products that be used as offerings for Aggayu include male goats, roosters, and guinea hens. Among fruits, mangoes, and bananas can be offered. With his feasting being celebrated July 25th, he also likes to have a dry white wine. Cornmeal porridge can also be offered to Aggayu with okra. This combination is known as Amala ila is one of the most favorite things he likes to eat.

Yemaya: The Mother Spirit

Yemeya is often also spelled as Yemoja, Yemanja, Lemanja or even Yemalla. Yemeya literally means "Mother of Water". Even though she is the Goddess of the vast open oceans and seas, she is also worshipped near lakes, wells or lagoons. Anywhere there is water; Yemeya is likely to be present. In West Africa, they worship Yemeya as a river deity, but in Brazil and Cuba, they worship her only as a sea/ocean Goddess. This mother spirit has a soft place in her heart for all the women of the world, especially pregnant women. It takes a lot to anger this Goddess because she doesn't get easily riled up. But when she does, you should expect a huge hurricane your way. She is quite loving but she is very powerful.

Yemeya loves her children and cares a lot for them. Their sorrow is almost as if it is Yemeya's sorrows. She protects women especially and cures infertility for women who cannot conceive a child. She is almost always involved during childbirth, child care, parenting, healing, love, and conception. Yemeya is also often depicted as a mermaid with 2 tails who is associated with the moon, water, and feminine mysteries. According to a Yoruba Pataki, when Yemeya's waters broke, it caused such a great flood that the water bodies on earth were created and that she gave birth to many human beings from her womb. In some cultures, Yemeya is also known to have given birth to the sun, moon, stars and many Orishas. She will unleash her wrath upon anyone who threatens her children.

According to Yoruba patakis and myths, when the slaves were transported across the oceans, it was Yemeya who protected and nurtured them. It was Yemeya who looked after them. She is the wife of Obatala, the chief, and the judge. Yemeya also often gets depressed over her children. However, she is a stylish Goddess and despises gaudy things. Which is why in Brazil, the worshippers throw a huge feast for this Goddess. On 2nd of February, everyone dresses up in white and goes down to the ocean to send her gifts and offerings on boats.

Yemeya's offerings should be laid out in a stylish setting. Seafood on a gold or silver plate, a fruit basket, and some excellent white wine are known to be the best way to please this stylish Goddess. What pleases her, even more, is if you donate to a family or children's charity or help a single mom. Yemeya also loves foamy lattes.

Apart from the oceans and large water bodies, Yemeya can be found at weddings, maternity wards or daycare centers.

Yemeya is known to wear a dress with seven skirts that represent the seven seas. With her favorite colors being blue and white and her favorite animals are the peacocks and ducks. Her number is 7, to signify the seven seas. The tools of Yemeya are the boat steering wheel, oars, anchors, and machetes. Cowrie shells are known to represent her wealth.

Orunmila - Orisha of Wisdom

Also known as Orunla and Orula, Orunmila is regarded as the Orisha of wisdom. His celestial parents are Oroko and Alayeru; however, on earth, he was born to Obatala and Yemaya.

In Yoruba religion, Orunmila is known as the first prophet. He controls the birth of mankind and other species. Apart from that, he also controls their development and deaths. People believe he was sent as a great benefactor for the mankind. Using his prophecy, lfa, he can reveal the future secrets. Orunmila is also considered a great healer.

It is said when the universe was being created, Orunmila was witness to it. It is also said when a spirit is made alive in the human form and is choosing its destiny, Orunmila is witness to this. Thus, he knows the destiny of people and other species of the universe and can tell them about what the future holds for them.

The characteristics associated with Orunmila include intelligence and wisdom. It is believed that he has a vast knowledge of the aspects of human life and nature that are unknown to all. Furthermore, he also has ample knowledge of humanity and mankind's history. This is why, he is known as the governing Orisha; however, he hasn't received the guarding Orisha crown. He was renowned as a calm and wise Orisha. He was also a spiritual guide for people. He helped people to get inner peace and calmness.

The privileges and the powers he has been bestowed with i.e. to have an awareness of the origin of every being including the Orishas and oshas, he enjoys using them. This empowers him to make others aware of their future and the ways they can change it for the better. If a person refused to believe Orunmila or neglects their advice, whether he is an Orisha or man, they can face the wrath of the Osogbos. Osogbos is sent by Eshu, the assistance of Orunmila. The priests of Orunmila need to be the wisest of all, along with being most organized and spiritual.

Orunmila colors are yellow and green. Therefore, his followers are seen wearing robes in these colors. They are worn in honor of him. Furthermore, they also wear Orunmila necklaces and bracelets that have beads in green and yellow colors. Wearing these ornaments help to arouse his power.

When it comes to offerings for Orunmila, he likes eating coconut and white basil. In addition, black hen, deer, dove, and female goat can also be offered. Other foods that can be offered are sweet cakes and wines. October 4th is known as the feast day of Orunmila; hence, the offerings must be made on this day.

To sum it up, with the guidance of Orunmila and his insights, you can get to know about future secrets and shape your life the way you want.

FOUR

Initiations

With the strength of the Orishas being so great, one doesn't become initiated purely for money or power. Instead, initiations in Santeria encourage the individual to move forward in their lives, generally in specific courses and pass on the Ashe or the divine influence of the Orishas into your way of life. There are a number of stages of initiation, and the education you obtain increases as well as the pledge required of you by the Orishas and your Godparents.

Guerreros

First, an individual will typically receive their Guerreros or warriors and/or their elekes or Necklaces. Afterward, they may obtain La Mano de Orula or Hand of Orula. At which time the individual is ready, they may progress on into the kariocha or full initiation as a Santera or Santero if that is their direction in life. Ultimately, if the individual's symbol in their Mano de Orula signals for it they may be totally initiated as the Father of the Secrets or a Babalawo and perform as a High Priest.

Initiations are suggested according to the desires of the

individual as influenced by the Orishas themselves through divination.

The initiation of the Orisha Warriors or Guerreros, are the first who must accept any initiate in the religion. These only can be done by the priests of high rank, denominated Oluwos or Babalawos. They will actually receive several Orishas consisting of Eshu/Elegua, Ogun, Oshun, and Ochosi. These Orishas will reside near an individual's front door and will require to be taken charge of each Monday as well as whenever they request for something through divination. As their knowledge increases in the religion, the better they will be capable to act amidst these Orishas. Over the course, these initiates will be instructed how to give a coconut or ori to their Guerreros to ask them uncomplicated yes or no queries.

Eshu/Elegua has many ways or routes with various specialties for each direction. He is received so he can clear an individual's path in life and shut the doors to all the energies that may hurt them. Elegua can be received from Santeros or Babalawos. When Eshu is received from a Babalawo, divination is performed to establish which of all these paths of Eshu accompanies that individual and the mystery with which he is prepared differs for each passage. When they receive their Guerreros from a Santero, the path is not determined until they are initiated as a Santera or Santero if that is the path of the individual's life.

As Elegua opens a path, Ogun clears the way of interferences and gives the tools with each to form a better way of life. He is also a mighty defender who is ready and willing to take on all comers. Oshun represents the head and happiness, warning an individual if they are in jeopardy by falling over. Only the Babalawos know the mysteries of how to prepare Oshun properly.

Ochosi inspires individuals to seek for the wonderful qualities in their existence. He helps individuals to skirt stumbling into traps and to make sure you are never lost in life. He also comes to your service and ensures Justice is carried out when an individual is wronged or to fight for when falsely accused.

The Elekes

Getting your Elekes or necklace (which can also be a bracelet) is just the first step of the religion. It is the ceremonial introduction inside Santeria and toward a new consciousness as a follower regarding the Orishas. Only Santeras and Santeros can conduct this rite and this service cannot be given by Babalawos.

Receiving your Elekes puts you under the graces and security of the Orishas of your Godparents' and establishes you as a part of their Ile or Orisha House. It signifies the tearing away and discarding the former life from you and you starting your journey onto the path of the Orishas.

There are five Elekes that one gets when first going thru the levels of spiritual development within the paths of the Orishas. These bead necklaces can be worn by a man or a woman to help accomplish their intent for the obstacle at hand. You should arrange your necklaces on or remove them one at a time. This should be in the same sequence that you received them.

The service of receiving the elekes itself takes several hours as it is made up of many rites, and the new initiate should be ready to set aside a day for it as they will be required to go home and relax for the balance of the night. The beads are a channel to link you to the Orisha on an everyday basis. It's like a mini altar being fixed on your body.

Each Orisha owns an eleke of a specific color, pattern, and shape. The elekes must be worn around the neck or wrist. The elekes should not be kept in a pocket or purse or balled up. Care should be exercised that they remain untangled. If the elekes are not being worn or carried, they should be carefully stored in a white cloth or put in the Orisha's bowl. The elekes is handled with respect once an individual has received them. You should not wear them when you are engaging in sexual activities, going to bars and nightclubs, and of course, they also should not be worn while sleeping because they will break with the movements of a sleeping body during the night. Furthermore, they should not be worn in baths, showers or while washing in the ocean or river, since water will make the string that has received the ache to break.

No one should touch your elekes except for a priest. If your beads fall to the floor or someone other than a child touches your elekes, wash them off using cool spring water.

If the eleke breaks, pick up as many beads as you can and call your Padrino or Madrina. It breaking just may mean that the Orisha has disrupted energy that could have caused you harm or protected you from something. Get a reading and look into it as well as replacing them with new ones.

Hand of Orula

For men, this is known as Awofakan and Ikofa for women. The Mano de Orula is an initiation toward the experience of Ifa. This initiation will place the individual under the safeguard and care of Orula (Orunmila) and is an extremely significant service that lasts three days. Women who have received Ikofa are considered Apetebis or Wives of Orula and are looked upon as the elders of those men who have Awofakan since they have moved through more services and are better thoroughly initiated than the men. The reason for this is that some men may subsequently move on to be thoroughly initiated as Babalawos. During this service, the greatest types of divination utilized are the Table of Ifa and the Odu or Sign that occurs up will guide that individual for their entire life. This Odu, one of a possible 256, displays the initiates' direction in their way of life and provides guidance by which they can fulfill themselves and avoid misfortune.

Kariocha

Kariocha or making Ocha is the indoctrination as a full status Santera or Santero in Santeria. They can consult with clients, perform cleansings and other remedies, and perform initiations. They are also viewed as royalty in Santeria as they are deemed agents of the Orishas and are in the possession of the capability to work with the energies of those Orishas in full.

This initiation also entails a great lifelong commitment of the initiate. For instance, the initiated Santera or Santero must progress through a year-long ceremony that is extremely involved and requiring many Priests. They fix the Orishas on your head, and that way your guardian angel is with you to support and look after you and to draw you all the gifts they can in this world.

There are many reasons individuals make the Saint. Sometimes for health reasons, an individual must carry out the Saint so that the individual's guardian angel can drive away any serious illness that medical society cannot. Often an individual gets the Saint because the Orishas wish for one to develop into a priest or priestess so they may serve them and society.

A decision with Orunla has to be performed to establish which Ebbo or cleansing should be given before the services start and in addition any other significant services that might be suggested. After establishing the Saint, one is an Iyawo. Iyawo signifies a bride in Yoruba. The initiate is recognized to be a bride to the Orisha whether the initiate is male or female. You are truly married to the Orisha. One must observe certain constraints for the period following the making of the Saint, one of which includes wearing white clothes. This is to safeguard the Iyawo, who is like a newborn baby spiritually and needs to be cared for from negative forces. Following making the Saint, one's Ashe grows with the years since one has Ocha crowned. Respect is of paramount interest in this religion, reverence for the elders, for godparents and reverence for the Orishas.

Making Ifa

Ifa is not only the greatest form of divination in the religion; it is the highest expression of La Regla Lucumi. Ifa teaches you that there are various reasons for initiation. This is the initiation service wherein an individual is totally initiated as a Babalawo or Father of the Secrets.

It is typical for many to enter into initiation in order to obtain the spiritual support and re-enforcement to achieve our dreams, goals, and aspirations. Reasons for initiation are extremely unique to the individual this is because we all have our own individual objectives, destinies and spiritual blueprint.

Determining this significant action starts and finishes perpetually with divination to see if this is the correct route for you to take, as well as to learn the needed pre-initiation actions to easily prepare you for this journey. It is severely selective and requires an extensive commitment in time, training and responsibility.

FIVE

The Sacrifice of Santeria

The Santeria religion is a kind of religion which was developed in the Caribbean among West African descendants. It is also known as Regla de Ocha or Lucumi. It is said to have been crafted out of the Yoruba religion of Ifa, and its sacred language is the Lucumi language which is a variety of the Yoruba language. The Santeria religion believes in the Orishas, which are the Yoruba deities. These Orishas are said to be many and perform various tasks as they were directed by the Olofin (God). The Santeria believes the Orishas are saints and the messengers of God. They also believe in the powers of the Orishas to perform all sorts of miracles if sacrifices (Ebbo) are performed to appease them.

Rituals in Santeria Religion

The Santeria church of the Orishas as their churches are called, engage in a lot of rituals. To the practitioners of this religion, sacrifice or Ebo are a very important cornerstone of the religion. They believe that the Orishas, which are the medium through which they speak to the almighty God used to be humans and even though they have been moved to the realm of immortality, they still have some human characteristics. They believe the Orishas get hungry just like humans from time to time, and for them to be able to perform effectively and help in propagating their messages to God, they need to be fed. As directed by divination (Ifa), a ritual is a way through which the Orishas can change peoples' lives for the better if done properly. Some of the ways by which rituals are done in the Santeria religion are as follow:

Addimu

These cooked offerings or addimu are a way of showing appreciation to the Orishas. The offerings are made up of the normal foods that the Lucumi (a variety of Yoruba language spoken in the Caribbean) people have in their diets. They are prepared and served to the various Orishas as they desire. It should be noted that different Orishas have different preferences when it comes to cooked meals and the practitioners know this very well. For example, Chango may prefer amala and ewedu, while Ogun tends to prefer Egusi and Iyan. To have a truly acceptable offering, these specifications must be adhered to.

Isogui

This involves the use of fruits; isogui is another type of offering to the Orishas. It should be noted too that each Orisha has their own preferences when it comes to fruits. It is advisable to ask the diviners when one don't know, so as to make the right and acceptable sacrifice. It is also advisable to take all the fruits to be used in the sacrifice from one tree or buy it in one store so as to make it more acceptable.

Eyebale

Perhaps the most important sacrifices or Ebbos in the Santeria religion is the blood sacrifice. This is regarded as a culture passed from hand to hand from the proponents of the religion in the old Yoruba Empire of West Africa and which must be adhered to at all times. It is said that the most important sacrifices must always involve blood. The blood used in these sacrifices is from animals. These animals are mostly the animals found on farms like roosters, chickens, sheep, goats, pigeons, etc. In killing the animals for sacrifice, Santeria religion advises great care of the animal so that the sacrifice can be accepted. For example, an animal that is to be used for sacrifice must be well fed and taken care of prior to the time of using it, and when it comes to slaughtering the animal, it is advised that the animal be slaughtered in a humane way that would make it be unconscious before being slaughtered by a knife.

Why do Santeria Sacrifice Animals?

The Santeria religion is totally immersed in the beliefs of its ancestors. The ancestors or progenitors of the early Ifa religion where Santeria took most of its principle from believe in the greater good of things and the instructions of the Orishas. They believe that offering animals to the Orishas according to the instructions of the Oracle helps in fostering a great relationship with them. This process is said to bring the worshippers closer to the Orishas and in return, the Orishas would help the worshippers out of any problem by helping them intercede with the almighty God. Also, they believe blood sacrifice is a way of having communions with the Orishas. When an animal is killed for a sacrifice, the Orishas only drink the blood and not the flesh of the animal. The flesh is then cooked and eaten by the worshippers of the various Orishas. By doing this, the worshippers believe they are dining with the Orishas and they would tend to attain some spiritual cleansing according to the powers of the Orishas. These sacrifices are performed at landmark events like weddings, naming ceremony, death and they are also used for healing. The belief of the Santeria is that the religion would die without the blood sacrifice.

Is It Possible To Sacrifice Without Animals?

The quick and the right answer is it is not possible. This is because every religion is based on strong and core principles upon which they should operate. Moving away from such principles would do nothing but to end the religion. The practitioners of the Santeria religion have come out to say that the most important aspect of their religion is the animal sacrifice. What this means is, without it, the religion would die a natural death. Imagine Christianity without evangelism or Islam without Salat? It is the same with Santeria religion. They have taken pride in following the laid down rules of their progenitors in the past, and stopping animal sacrifice would be synonymous with throwing away every principle they have held dear in the past. Also, they have been able to maneuver their ways from the wrath of legal authorities as it relates to the using of an animal as sacrifices. In the case of 'Church of Lucumi Babalu Aye v. the City of Hialeah in 1993', the USA Supreme Court ruled that it is constitutional for Santeria worshippers to kill animals for their rituals. This could have been the major impediment to their cause, but since that was achieved way back, it is safe to say, the Santeria religion would not even consider other options as it comes to animal sacrifices.

SIX

Divination Practices in Santeria

A fundamental part of Santeria is divination. Those who adhere to the practices of Santeria rely on the guidance and advice they obtain from their deceased ancestors and the Orishas to help them decide and move through challenging stages. Divination is a sacred practice that embodies sanctified tools in its use.

Few individuals have the spiritual strength to develop into a consultant in divination. These practices involve comprehensive instruction and follow specific procedures. Priests and priestesses, known as Olorichas, work for years to hone their skills to talk with the spirits to get answers to problems or direction concerning particular circumstances.

Dilogun: The Cowrie Shells

Cowrie shells are small seashells, with a closed top and an opened bottom, seen as a mouth. These shells became a favored medium in divination ceremonies generations ago. It is suggested these sacred shells are the passageway through which we can connect the realm of the ancestors. This world carries the vast wisdom and knowledge we otherwise could not utilize.

Various cultures maintain the magic appears from its parallel to a half-open eye. Other groups perceive a correlation between the cowrie and female genitalia, and they have developed into a symbol of fertility.

They use sixteen cowrie shells during a reading. The cowrie shells chosen for a reading are called a dilogun. Considered to be the mouthpieces of the Orishas, the Santero or Santera will listen to what the cowrie shells convey to them.

With the Santero or Santera beginning by sprinkling water around where the reading will take place. This is to reinvigorate the home and get rid of negative energy; to strengthen the dilogun, and to cleanse the individual requesting guidance. A sequence of pleas and dedications in the ancient dialect of Yoruba will follow.

They tossed the shells onto a grass mat, table, sacred cloth or wooden board and then interpreted based on how they landed. The healer or priest would infer meanings based on the grouping, position, and inclination of the shells.

An individual who's going through some kind of obstacle, who suffers anxiety or concern about a situation will ask for a Santero or Santera to receive advice and help. A Santero or Santera will disclose if the client has blessings (ire) or obstructions (osorbo) in their life at the present moment. If there is osorbo, the Santero or Santera will figure out where it comes from and what causes it, and offer remedies for how to remove it. If there's ire, the client will learn what to do to make sure the blessings continue. A Santero or Santera can touch on many facets of a person's life. This may consist of money, work, success, physical, mental, and emotional health. Anything that might impact on the client's life. It combines practical advice mixed in with metaphysical and spiritual teachings, to help the client bring his life back into harmony and live the life they were meant to have.

Throwing cowrie shells has long been a tradition in insight, and one rich in history and tribal heritage.

Obi: The Coconut

Unlike the cowrie shells, Obi or the coconut in Lucumi is one of the simplest forms of divination that an Oloricha can do. It is never applied to perform a particular reading for an individual. Instead, the coconut is used through various rituals, ceremonies, and events. The coconut is most frequently used to establish whether an Orisha or saint is happy with a ritual, service or offering. If they bless the occasion, all is well. Any of the Orishas, as well as the spirits of the dead, may be consulted through the coconut. They often call the coconut divination technique, Obi.

Obi is sacred and must be used with respect. The Oloricha is required to open a fresh coconut using a mallet or a machete. This divination method requires four coconut rinds of equal size.

Using prayers and following ritual protocol, the Oloricha throws the pieces of obi to the floor to get answers to yes or no questions. This kind of ritual is performed to determine out what tribute the Orishas require, where to put it, and if they're pleased with it once it has been offered.

Because every rind is brown on one side while white on the opposite, there are five distinguished patterns which can appear.

Four white coconut sides up is Alafia. The answer to a question with this result would be a resounding yes.

Three white coconut sides up with one dark side is Etawa. The answer to a question with this result would be that the answer is unknown and vague, and the coconuts must be cast again.

Two white coconut sides up with two dark sides is Ejife.

The answer to a question with this result would be, yes. All things are correct and blessed.

One white side coconut up with three dark sides is Okanran. The answer to a question with this result would be that before a blessing can occur, the circumstance needs to be fixed. A definite sign of something is wrong.

Four dark coconut sides up is Oyekun. The answer to a question with this result would be that this is a very serious sign something, many things, are not right.

SEVEN

Spells

Santeria spells can be of varied natures and can differ as different desires of specific people, the shared part of all the spell creation under Santeria religion is about performing the rites and offerings specific to the specific Orishas and receiving the Ashe from them to create a successful goal in casting the spell.

These spells can be used for finding love, eliminating problems connected to survival, commitment from your companion, etc.

All these spells are cast entirely by the Santera or Santero and you would likewise locate a Babalawo taking part in the spell ritual, but if you adhere to a few steps properly even you can cast Santeria spells by yourself, but again to obtain an immediate result and perfect result you should always rely on a spell cast by the Santera or Santero.

You must first recognize which deity to honor and pray to, then you should choose the specific things which the Orisha claims as their and present it to them. Once the deity is pleased with your offering, you will receive the power of fulfilling your intention. Remember you can wish only once and be extremely precise, since a wish cannot be copied or be in general.

After your wish is granted, make certain to acknowledge the Orisha and maintain a note of the progress of the spells results.

A little better understanding on how to cast the spell, for the spell here you would need to please Elegba deity of Santeria ritual. If you have the slightest plan of hurting someone, then the Orisha will never help you accomplish what you are searching for.

Santeria Money Spell

This spell is meant for individuals who are regular lotto players.

Yellow Flowers
1 Yellow Candle
1 Green Candle
11x14 Yellow or Green Poster Board
Black Marker
Ruler or Straight Edge

On one short, side in a grid pattern, write all the numbers in random order that are used in your lottery game. On the other side write the date when you wish to play the game, then place the poster on the altar, covering it with the yellow flowers hiding the numbers. Light the yellow candle and the green candle and request for the numbers of your lottery game would appear as winning numbers on the very date you have previously written. Hold both candles together in your hand and allow twenty-one drops of wax from each candle to fall on the poster board. Discard the flowers from the paper revealing only the winning numbers.

Passion and Lust Spell

2 Red Candles
Photo of Yourself
Photo of Your Love
Construction Paper Red Heart
Deity: Oshun or Chango
When to Perform: Friday for Oshun, Tuesday for Chango

Clean and fix the candles. Write your goals, wishes, and intentions on the back of the heart. Indicate as precisely as imaginable. Make your request to Oshun or Chango. Request for everything you want. Be frank and straightforward. Be clear and work in peace with the universe.

Place the two red candles about twelve inches apart with the photos in the center, within the two candles. Make certain that the photos touch each other. Place the heart on top of each photo.

Burn the candles. Be assured that the flame has a connection amidst the spiritual plane. Let the candles burn for seven minutes. Push the two candles two inches closer before extinguishing them.

Thank Oshun or Chango for assisting you.

The following day at the same time, repeat by burning candles for seven minutes. Perform this each night for a sum of seven nights. On the seventh night, make certain both candles are touching the photos and the heart. Allow the candles burn out.

Get the heart and the photos and placed them in a secure spot and store them till your goals, intentions, and hopes have come true.

When whatever you have requested come to you, be certain to acknowledge both the deity and Oshun or Chango for your success.

Return to photos and heart to nature by burning, them burying them, or throwing them into running water, such as an ocean, lake, or river.

. . .

Commitment Spell

2 Pink Candles
Photo of Yourself
Photo of Your Love
Construction Paper Red Heart
Deity: Oshun
When to Perform: Friday

Clean and fix the candles. Write your goals, wishes, and intentions on the back of the heart. Imply as precise as imaginable. Make your request to Oshun. Request for everything you want. Be frank and straightforward. Be clear and work in peace with the universe.

Place the two pink candles around twelve inches apart with the photos in the center, within the two candles. Make certain that the photos touch each other. Place the heart on top of each photo.

Burn the candles. Be assured that the flame has a connection amidst the spiritual plane. Let the candles to burn for seven minutes. Push the two candles two inches closer before extinguishing them.

Thank Oshun for assisting you.

The following day at the same time, repeat by burning candles for seven minutes. Perform this each night for a sum of seven nights. On the seventh night, make certain both candles are touching the photos and the heart. Allow the candles to burn out.

Get the heart and the photos and placed them in a secure spot and store them till your goals, intentions, and hopes have come true.

When whatever you have requested come to you, be certain to acknowledge both the deity and Oshun for your success.

Return to photos and heart to nature by burning, them burying them, or throwing them into running water, such as an ocean, lake, or river.

EIGHT

Terms Used In Santeria

Santeria is a religion that incorporates beliefs from Roman Catholic Christianity and Yoruba. It is performed chiefly in West Africa and the Caribbean. Many Puerto Ricans, Dominicans, and Cubans practice Santeria. Like any religion, it includes unique rituals, ceremonies, and, of course, terminology. Here's a brief guide to some of the terms you might encounter in Santeria. Remember, there are hundreds of words connected to this religion, so these are just some basics!

A
  Abbita: Devil.
  Abiku: When a spirit wishes to come back to the world and kills many children or a name for children prematurely marked by death.
  Aberinkulo: To terrify the dead.
  Aboricha: Someone which is partly although not fully initiated into Santeria. For instance, an individual who has accepted the warrior's or an eleke from a godparent during a formal ritual.
  Achabba: A metal charm or talisman bracelet/anklet

with weapons, keys, tools, machetes, plus other items of metal dangling from it. It is sometimes carried by priests of Ogun.

Acho: A bit of material presented to an Orisha as an offering, or utilized in a cleansing ritual.

Achupua: The Moon.

Addimu: Type of ebbo or offering made to the Orishas, consisting of uncooked or cooked foods. Every Orisha has his or her favorite foods.

Ahijada/Ahijado: Godchild in the Santeria religion.

Aja: A broom fashioned from palm fibers customarily used by Babalu Aye. It clears away illness and negative energy.

Aleyo: A stranger to the religion. An individual who has not accepted the warriors, elekes or anything else from a godparent.

Amala: One of Chango's favorite foods. It is a thick stew dish made of cornmeal, okra and sometimes mutton.

Ashe/Ache: Grace, blessing, good fortune. Ashe pa ti means "good luck."

Atana: A candle worked throughout a Santeria ceremony. Frequently two candles are used.

Aye: Earth, the section occupied by living beings.

B

Babaloricha/Babalocha: A Santera or Santero that has initiated others in the religion.

Babalawo: A priest of Orula; spiritual leader of the Regla de Ifa.

Bata/Tambores: Set of three sacred drums employed in ceremonies.

Bembe: Drumming ceremony in honor of the Orishas, also called a tambour in Cuba.

C

Caballo: Accurately, a horse. This word is utilized to define the individual who is possessed by an Orisha throughout a trance. The Orisha attaches to an individual and controls him or her as a channel to interact with others in the area.

Camino: Path or avatar of the Orisha. Most Orishas have many avenues, meaning they can choose various forms and be characterized in different forms. During initiation, when Santeros receive the Orishas, they see which directions their Orishas take.

Canastillero: In the past, a china cabinet where the soperas with the Orishas were held; today the canastillero can be any piece of furniture utilized as a shrine or altar in the home where the soperas of the Orishas are maintained.

Consulta/Registro: The divination method performed by a Babalawo or Santera or Santero for a client. With the use of the cowrie shells or epuele chain, the Orishas talk to the client.

D

Derecho: Payment to a Santero for a service. May also be a contribution to a godparent on the holiday of the godparent's initiation.

Dilogun: Cowrie shells that have been blessed for use by an Oloricha to interact with the Orishas.

E

Ebbo: Also spelled ebo. Sacrifice or offering made to an Orisha. Ebbo takes many forms and is normally determined through a consulta with the dilogun or epuele.

Ebbo Misi: A spiritual bath for protection or purification. May involve flowers, herbs, plants, cascarilla, cocoa butter, or additional ingredients defined by a consulta.

Efun/Cascarilla: Powder composed of finely ground white eggshells, utilized in various Santeria rituals.

Egun: The Ancestors or Spirits of the dead. Traditionally, egun are restricted to blood-relatives.

Eleke: Beaded necklace in the color of specific Orishas. The elekes are blessed and given by a godparent after a ceremony. They represent the Ashe of the Orisha and are sacred.

Emi: Sacred breath, what gives us life on earth.

Ekuele/Epuele: Used by a Babalawo for divination, it is a short chain to which 8 pieces of coconut shell have been attached. The Babalawo throws the ekuele and notes the patterns that fall.

Ella/Eya: Dried fish, used as an offering to some Orishas.

Eyioko: One of the odu concerning dilogun divination; it relates to the number 2.

Ewe: Grass herb used in Santeria ceremonies. Each Orisha is linked with numerous plants and herbs that are used to prepare omiero. Herbs can also be used for medicinal purposes. Can refer to the constraints people place on themselves on their time of Ita.

F

Foribale: The ceremonious tribute a practitioner of Santeria gives to the Orishas or frequently a godparent or respected elder; literally, it implies to bring the head to the ground. Depending on which Orisha controls the head of the Santero/a the person can lie face down with arms stretched back to the sides, or lie initially on the right side then the left side, with the arm crooked at the waist.

G

Guemilere: A celebration held in the worship of the

Orishas, not limited to initiates. The sacred Bata drums aren't used. There is usually drinking, eating and dancing, in excess to show gratitude to the Orishas for great prosperity.

I

Ibe Bae Tonu: A phrase used while invoking or vocalizing the name audibly of an ancestor who has departed; it's intended to honor the dead including wishing them the best in the next life.

Idde: A beaded bracelet carried by initiates in Santeria. The idde need to be blessed in a ceremony before it can be worn.

Igbodu: A sacred place where initiation into Santera takes place.

Iboru, Iboyo, Ibocheche: A greeting made by the Father of mysteries and secrets in commemoration of three women who saved the life of the Orula.

Iku: Death: The worst of the osorbos. Iku is sometimes symbolized and can roam on earth looking for individuals to bring into the domain of the dead.

Ile Ocha: A church or house of worship where the practitioners of Santeria conduct rituals.

Ire: Good energy, good luck, and blessings. Using the dilogun (shells) in divination, the Santero learns if his client's reading comes with ire or osorbos (bad luck).

Irosun: One of the odu of dilogun divination; corresponds to the number 4.

Iruke: Horsetail constructed into a short whip, which is used by Obatala and Oya while dancing. It's used to expel away negative energies. Obatala's is white and Oya's is black.

Ita: Ceremony where you speak of the past, present and future.

Iwa: A human being's nature. Iwa rere is a good character. It's something we should all aim for.

Iworo: Another name for Santero.

Iyabo/Iyawo: A novice initiate in Santeria. In most circumstances, this term lasts one year, plus the iyabo has many restraints on his/her behavior during that time.

Iyaboraje: The one-year interval following initiation into Santeria.

K

Kariocha: The initiation rite in Santeria. In Cuba, individuals also apply the words "hacer santo" (to make saint) and "asentar santo" (to seat the saint) to refer to initiation.

Kincamache: For health. Generally used as a phrase to wish for good health.

L

Letra: The letter or symbol marked in divination by the manner the shells land on the mat. The letra is similarly called an odu or oddun. The letra brings with it a complex array of patakis, pieces of advice, proverbs, and messages from the Orishas, and recommended contributions that can be made to the Orishas or spirits of the dead (the egun) to provide good fortune.

Limpieza: Spiritual bath and/or Spiritual cleansing.

Lucumi/Lukumi: Deals with to the Yoruba individuals who were taken to Cuba as slaves and their descendants. Santeria is also identified as the Lucumi religion.

M

Madrina: Godmother in the Santeria religion.

Mariwo: Palm fronds, fibers or stalks.

Moyugbar/Modyuba/Moyuba: To pray to the ancestors and the Orishas before any rite, to petition for permission, blessings, and to show respect to godparents.

O

Obara: One of the odu of dilogun divination; associated with the number 6.

Obi: Coconut. Used in many Santeria ceremonies, or as a tribute to an Orisha.

Ocana: One of the odu of dilogun divination; associated with the number 1.

Ocha: A shortened form of Orisha.

Oche/Oshe: One of the odu of dilogun divination; associated with the number 5.

Ochinchin: Oshun's favorite food. Ochinchin is made with eggs cooked with dried shrimp and chard.

Odi: One of the odu of dilogun divination; associated with the number 3.

Odu/Oddun: The letter or symbol identified in divination by the design the shells drop on the cloth. Also known as letra.

Ofoche: Magickal powders used during witchcraft.

Ogo: Witchcraft. One of the roots of osorbo.

Ogunda: One of the odu of dilogun divination; associated with the number 3.

Ofun: One of the odu of dilogun divination; associated with the number 10.

Ojuani: One of the odu of dilogun divination; associated with the number 11.

Olofi/Olofin: The supreme god. The King of Kings.

Oloricha: An initiated priest or priestess of Santeria. May also be known as a Santera (female) or Santero (male).

Olubata: The artist who plays the intricate patterns and melodies on the batas in the worship of the Orishas.

Omi: Water offered to the Orishas as a drink. Omi tuto implies "fresh water."

Omiero: Holy water blended with herbs and additional natural elements, used throughout the initiation service to birth the Orishas. The omiero is made in a complicated function following the direction of an elder, followed by petitions.

Omilasa: Holy water, of a Catholic church. The fact is that in Cuba, Santeria has combined aspects of Catholicism. It's generally considered that holy water from a church has therapeutic as well as protective powers.

Oriate: Santera/o who is viewed in the society as a leader of services. To become an oriate entails several years of intense learning. The oriate leads and directs initiation rituals. An oriate is similarly called Oba (chief).

Orun: Heaven.

Osa: An odu of dilogun divination; associated with the number 9.

Osorbo/Osobbo: Bad luck, obstructions, defeat. Within divination, using the dilogun, the Santero decides if his client's reading comes with osorbo or ire (blessings.)

Ota/Otan: A rock or stone which symbolically accepts the Ashe of an Orisha through the initiation service; typically the stones are held in soup tureens or soperas.

Oti: Sugarcane alcohol applied to various Santeria services.

Owo: Money, wealth, good luck in business. A form of ire.

Oyugbona: The secondary godmother or godfather in an initiation service. The oyugbona possesses most of the trust of caring for the brand-new initiate throughout the week-long initiation rite. Also known as a type of Santeria priestess.

P

Padrino: Godfather in the Santeria religion.

Pataki: Religious narrative or tale involving God, the

Orishas, the formation of the earth, or other significant spiritual issues. Part of divination systems, Patakis generally exist in oral form and are explained to godchildren by the godparents. They can be applied through a consulta to represent a moralistic situation.

R

Regla de Ifa: Ifa relates to a faction of male priests which are dedicated to Orula. Ifa is corresponding to but not technically a piece of Regla de Ocha. Some males are received leading into Regla de Ocha and subsequently move into Regla de Ifa. In Cuba, Ifa is solely for males.

Regla de Ocha: Ocha is a shorter form of Orisha. Regla de Ocha is another name for Santeria. Regla means to control or manner of working out something.

Rogacion de Cabeza: Head cleansing, a rite carried out to support, calm, or look after the head (ori).

S

Sarayeyeo: Purification ceremony that is performed with the follower of Santeria at the foot of an Orisha

Sopera: Soup dish or tureen, employed to house the ota (stones) that symbolically illustrate the Orishas on a home shrine or altar. Originally the Orishas were placed in gourds but in Cuba through the 19th century, it became popular to place them in ceramic soperas and to keep the soperas in a china cabinet, sideboard or buffet in the home.

Suyere: The song or prayer that praises an Orisha.

U

Unle/Eyeunle: An odu of dilogun divination; associated with the number 8.

W

Warriors: Refers to Elegua, Ogun, Ochosi, and Oshun. These four Orishas collectively are called the warriors. It's natural to receive the warriors before becoming completely initiated into Santeria. Those who possess the warriors are medio sentados or half-way introduced into Santeria. Also known as Guerreros.

Conclusion

As your studies develop in Santeria, you'll come across other followers of the church and you're going to learn about varying styles and inconsistencies in the approach people follow the teaching. Maintain a clear understanding and try not to judge others in the process of your individual learning.

Adhere to the way things are performed in your god-family. You'll develop in your neighborhood, learn and form respectful bonds with your god-family. As you move your way in Santeria you'll see just how best to function as a family, how to praise the Orishas, worship your ancestors, and your family by your actions and in how you manage yourself in life.

Writers, musicians, artists, dancers, and composers have discovered in the Orisha tradition sources of African style and dignity. It is safe to say that Orisha traditions will continue to expand and be identified as one of the leading African contributions to world culture.

Remember, virtually a million Cubans fled the island after the Cuban Revolution of 1959, and extended across various localities, including significant parts of America. Many followers have received public appreciation for their spiritual achievements. Given the past of the Santeria religion, their

Conclusion

customs and practices are retained and passed on personally, as opposed to other religions that use texts and documents as their instrument of safeguard.

As of now, thousands of individuals accept this religion in the United States, with the figure simply building every year.

About the Author

Monique Joiner Siedlak is a writer, witch, and warrior on a mission to awaken people to their greatest potential through the power of storytelling infused with mysticism, modern paganism, and new age spirituality. At the young age of 12, she began rigorously studying the fascinating philosophy of Wicca. By the time she was 20, she was self-initiated into the craft, and hasn't looked back ever since. To this day, she has authored over 40 books pertaining to the magick and mysteries of life.

To find out more about Monique Joiner Siedlak artistically, spiritually, and personally, feel free to visit her **official website**.

www.mojosiedlak.com

- facebook.com/mojosiedlak
- twitter.com/mojosiedlak
- instagram.com/mojosiedlak
- pinterest.com/mojosiedlak
- bookbub.com/authors/monique-joiner-siedlak

Other Books by Monique Joiner Siedlak

Practical Magick
Wiccan Basics
Candle Magick
Wiccan Spells
Love Spells
Abundance Spells
Herb Magick
Moon Magick
Creating Your Own Spells
Gypsy Magic

Personal Growth and Development
Creative Visualization
Astral Projection for Beginners
Meditation for Beginners
Manifesting With the Law of Attraction
Reiki for Beginners
Stress Management

The Yoga Collective
Yoga for Beginners
Yoga for Stress
Yoga for Back Pain
Yoga for Weight Loss
Yoga for Flexibility

Yoga for Advanced Beginners

Yoga for Fitness

Yoga for Runners

Yoga for Energy

Yoga for Your Sex Life

Yoga: To Beat Depression and Anxiety

Yoga for Menstruation

A Natural Beautiful You

Creating Your Own Body Butter

Creating Your Own Body Scrub

Creating Your Own Body Spray

THANK YOU FOR READING MY BOOK! I REALLY APPRECIATE ALL OF YOUR FEEDBACK AND I LOVE TO HEAR WHAT YOU HAVE TO SAY. PLEASE LEAVE YOUR REVIEW AT YOUR FAVORITE RETAILER!

www.ingramcontent.com/pod-product-compliance
Lightning Source LLC
Chambersburg PA
CBHW071456070426
42452CB00040B/1537